Original title:
Cedar Serenades

Copyright © 2025 Creative Arts Management OÜ
All rights reserved.

Author: Levi Montgomery
ISBN HARDBACK: 978-1-80567-195-4
ISBN PAPERBACK: 978-1-80567-494-8

Echoes in the Forest Shade

In the shade, the squirrels chatter,
As the birds sing a tune, quite the clatter.
A raccoon dances, oh what a sight,
While the deer roll their eyes in fright.

A frog leaps high with a froggy cheer,
The trees giggle, 'Oh dear, oh dear!'
Branches sway to the rhythm of glee,
Nature's party, come join us, you'll see!

Lullabies of the Ancient Boughs

The wise old trees hum a soft tune,
While the owls wink at the rising moon.
Worms in the ground dance a wiggly jig,
And the ants boast of their mighty gig.

A chipmunk naps with dreams full of nuts,
While the wind tells secrets with little huffs.
A squirrel snickers at the slipping hare,
While shadows chuckle without a care.

The Treetops' Secret Choir

The treetops buzz with a whispery sound,
The choir of leaves is joyfully found.
A parrot learned a silly old rhyme,
As he sings, 'I feel just sublime!'

Bumblebees bop in their golden suits,
While flower petals dance in their boots.
The sunbeams join the cheerful refrain,
And the forest keeps laughing again and again!

Rhythms of the Resinous Breaths

Pine cones play drums on the forest floor,
While woodpeckers giggle at each little score.
The saplings sway, feeling quite grand,
As the breeze twirls them, hand in hand.

A gopher pops up, with a wink and a grin,
Says, 'You should see my cartwheel spin!'
The moss joins in for a slippery dance,
Nature's oddities—oh, take a chance!

Chords of Bark and Bough

In the woods where the squirrels play,
They gather nuts in a funny way.
With acorns tossed like a game of ball,
They all laugh loudly, its a nutty brawl.

A chipmunk sings a sweet little tune,
While a raccoon dances beneath the moon.
The trees hum along, swaying in glee,
Nature's band plays, come sing with me!

The Sanctuary of Saplings

Tiny trees with a giggle and grin,
Frolicking in the soft, warm wind.
They wear hats made of leaves and twigs,
And sway to the beat, do little jigs.

A skunk tells jokes till the sun's in sight,
While rabbits hop and join the delight.
In this haven where laughter grows,
The saplings thrive, with fun in their prose!

In the Arms of the Wooded Haven

Cuddled in branches, away from the fuss,
A hedgehog snores, creating quite a fuss.
Branches tickle as they sway to and fro,
In cozy nooks, they nap, don't you know?

A bear shares stories with great delight,
Of fish caught under the starry night.
Laughter echoes through the leaves so green,
In the woods, joy reigns, a silly scene!

Sonnet of the Starlit Canopy

Beneath the stars, the critters convene,
With fireflies dancing, the trees are a screen.
A raccoon recites with a twist of his tail,
While owls hoot softly, as if on a trail.

The moon plays the piano, soft and bright,
As all the night creatures gather in sight.
In playful jest, they share tales untold,
Under the starlit canopy, joy unfolds.

The Stillness Between the Leaves

In the breeze, the branches sway,
A squirrel lost his acorn ballet.
He twirled and spun, what a sight,
Nutty chaos, a comical fright.

A crow cawed loud, with quite the flair,
As a chipmunk fumed, pulling its hair.
"Stop the racket!" the squirrel cried,
While all the woodlands just sighed.

Folklore of the Woodland Dawn

A rabbit wore a top hat grand,
He tipped it low, just as he planned.
"Good morning, folks!" he did declare,
While the owls squinted in their lair.

A fox played jazz on a tinny drum,
The deer swayed close, saying, "What fun!"
They partied on 'til dawn did break,
Until the woodpecker yelled, "For Pete's sake!"

The Tranquil Symphony of Spruce

The wind whistled a silly tune,
While raccoons danced beneath the moon.
A porcupine joined, looking quite dapper,
In his spiky coat, he was a show-stopper.

The sloth cheered, "Let's move it, please!"
But just hung tight on the nearest trees.
"Pick up the pace!" the otter teased,
As the forest giggled, a bit bemused.

Enchanted by the Timbered Sky

A bat wore glasses, read the news,
While owls pondered, sipping their brews.
"Who's got the scoop?" one said with glee,
The answer echoed, "Not a tree!"

The sun peeked out, a mischievous sprite,
Joking with shadows, playing all night.
With laughter ringing, all took a bow,
In the timbered sky, oh, what a wow!

The Fable of the Whispering Pines

In the woods where whispers dwell,
The trees tell tales with a swell.
One pine said, "I'm quite a catch!"
Another laughed, "You're just a witch!"

A squirrel danced on branches high,
While birds just giggled, oh my my!
They mimicked each jester's jest,
Echoing laughter from the nest.

Resonance of the Evergreen Night

Under stars, the tall trees sway,
They plot and plan some mischief play.
A branch teased, "Hey, look at me!"
While roots just rolled, "Let's wait and see!"

The owls hooted, what a sight!
As branches twirled in pure delight.
Each rustle brought a tiny cheer,
The night was fun, that much was clear.

Songs of the Twilit Glade

In twilight's glow, the laughter spilled,
A fox brought jokes, the crowd was thrilled.
"Why don't trees ever play charades?"
"Because they'd just leaf, in silly raids!"

The rabbits hopped in merry tune,
While fireflies danced beneath the moon.
Each leaf whispered, a giggle or two,
In a glade where laughter always grew.

The Poetry of Wood and Wind

Where wood meets wind, a melody spins,
The branches chuckle as the log grins.
A trunk proclaimed, "I stand so tall!"
But the wind replied, "You're just a wall!"

The logs conspired, the knots took bets,
"Who can make the best sound effects?"
With the breeze carrying tales so wild,
The forest giggled, just like a child.

Quaking Reflections in the Meadow

In the meadow, grasshoppers dance,
Wobbling like they lost their pants.
Butterflies giggle, take to the sky,
As a squirrel wonders, 'Oh me, oh my!'

Sunflowers turn, they can't hold still,
Chasing the sun up over the hill.
Frogs croak jokes from beneath the leaves,
While a bee buzzes, "Leave me, please!"

The Wind's Untamed Melody

The wind whistles tunes in quirky tones,
Like a cat on a fence with funny bones.
Trees sway and twist to the breeze's tease,
While an owl blinks, "Well, that was a breeze!"

As the branches shake, whispers of laughter,
Squirrels tell tales of disaster after.
Raccoons roll in leaves like a silly parade,
Under the moon, fresh mischief is made!

Pinecone Whispers at Dusk

Pinecones chatter, plotting their schemes,
Dreaming of glory in nutty dreams.
A fox prances in with a curious glance,
"Who needs a party when we have a dance?"

Mice join the fun, in little bow ties,
Twirling and spinning, oh what a surprise!
Laughter echoes beneath the tall trees,
As the night brings gossip on the soft breeze.

Emerald Dreams in Whispering Woods

In the emerald woods, the trees are alive,
Frogs in tuxedos prepare to dive.
A rabbit hops in with a quirky grin,
"Join me, my friends, let the party begin!"

Fireflies blink like stars in a row,
Joining the chorus, putting on a show.
With laughter and bites of unconventional pie,
The woods hum with fun as the hours fly by!

Melodies Beneath the Canopy

Under boughs so green and wide,
Squirrels dance with nuts to hide.
Beneath the leaves, a melody,
Chirps of frogs sing harmony.

Raccoons wear their masks with glee,
Playing tricks on you and me.
The owls hoot a silly tune,
As the stars begin to swoon.

A woodpecker finds his beat,
Tapping rhythms, oh so sweet.
While the breeze joins in the fun,
Nature's party just begun!

Laughter echoes through the trees,
As branches sway with playful ease.
Every critter joins the song,
In this world where all belong.

Lullabies of the Tall Pines

Pines stand tall, oh what a sight,
Crickets chirp into the night.
With each breeze, a soft lullaby,
As fireflies start to fly high.

Beneath the stars, raccoons nest,
In furry coats, they look their best.
While owls wink from branches spry,
Singing softly, 'Oh my, my!'

A badger hums a nightly tune,
Joining with the crooning moon.
Nature sways with gentle grace,
All creatures find their perfect space.

Lullabies float through the air,
Swaying leaves without a care.
In slumber deep, the woods abide,
Dreaming dreams where fun can't hide.

Echoes of the Woodland Breeze

In the woods, the breeze takes flight,
Tickling leaves with pure delight.
A chipmunk laughs, a quick, short cheer,
Echoes bounce from ear to ear.

The branches wave, a silly show,
While dandelions dance below.
Squirrels mimic the breeze's laugh,
Taking turns for a photo graph!

A deer trips over fallen logs,
Stumbling by the giggling frogs.
The rustling leaves play a prank,
As shadows join an impish rank.

In the wood, the fun won't cease,
Even creatures join for peace.
With every echo, joy is found,
In the laughter that surrounds.

Harmonies of the Forest Floor

On the ground, the leaves do cheer,
As mushrooms pop up, loud and clear.
A rabbit hops, a comical sight,
Bouncing around with pure delight.

Underfoot, the critters play,
Chasing shadows through the day.
A toad croaks, trying to impress,
While ants march in a tiny dress.

With every step, a hidden tune,
Drifting softly under the moon.
Nature's giggles fill the space,
In this ever-changing place.

Harmony beckons, old and wise,
While every creature's filled with surprise.
On the forest floor, we're never bored,
With melodies that can't be ignored.

Enchanted Echoes of the Earth

In the forest, whispers play,
Raccoons singing all the way.
Squirrels dance, a furry show,
While the pine trees giggle low.

A frog hops in a jaunty stride,
Chasing bugs and taking pride.
The owls hoot with perfect grace,
As if they've won a nutty race.

Among the roots, a fox does prance,
Stumbling in a clumsy dance.
Nature laughs, a lively scene,
Where every creature's bright and keen.

Each sound a joke, each breeze a jest,
This woodland life is truly blessed.
Laughter rises, soft and clear,
Echoing far, for all to hear.

Nature's Timeless Ballad

A worm in tails, a quirky sight,
Trying to wiggle, oh what a plight!
Ladybugs giggle as they fly,
Sipping nectar, oh my, oh my!

The ants parade, a marching band,
With tiny hats and plucky stand.
Bumbles buzz with silly flair,
Making honey like it's rare.

Trees sway gently, join the tune,
Their leaves flutter like a cartoon.
Insects chirp, creating beats,
A herbal waltz that never repeats.

The sun peeks in with playful rays,
Joining in this nature's craze.
With every note, the world reminds,
Life is music, and joy entwines.

The Dance of the Leafy Troop

Leaves twirl down, a dizzy flight,
While chipmunks dance throughout the night.
They joke around, such lively sprites,
Tickling each other, oh what delights!

Branches shake in laughter fit,
As pinecones tumble, just a bit.
Mice in sneakers, running fast,
Hidden treasures on the grass.

In every nook, a wink is passed,
Nature's humor unsurpassed.
The breeze whispers silly puns,
As sunlight plays, all laughs and runs.

Frogs croak jokes, a ribbit cheer,
Echoes bouncing, far and near.
This leafy gang knows just the role,
Planting giggles in every soul.

A Tapestry of Needles and Air

Pine needles sprinkle like confetti,
As birds chirp tunes that are quite petty.
They brag about their soaring flight,
While groundhogs hide with sheer delight.

A deer prances, doing a jig,
Celebrating each win with a big wig.
Under the boughs, a rabbit fell,
Convinced he can dance quite well.

Nature's canvas swirls with glee,
Painting joy for you and me.
Squirrels chat in tiny tones,
Planning pranks with little moans.

As dusk descends, the stars peek through,
The forest giggles—oh, who knew?
With every rustle, every breeze,
Life's a joke, a merry tease.

A Symphony of Saps and Streams

In the woods where laughter grows,
Trees tell tales in giggling throes.
Their sticky sap, a sweetened treat,
Turns every bark into a beat.

And squirrels wear their acorn hats,
While chatting up the nearby cats.
The rhythm flows, a playful dance,
Nature's jesters take a chance.

Old rocks chuckle, moss grows bright,
As birds belt tunes from morning light.
With every breeze, a chuckled song,
In this forest, we all belong.

So join the fun where laughter rings,
Among the branches, joy takes wings.
Let every twig and leaf conspire,
To weave a tune that won't expire.

Amongst the Pines, a Tale Unfolds

Between the trunks where shadows leap,
A drama stirs and creatures peep.
A pinecone rolls, its journey bold,
A comedy of nature's mold.

The owls wear glasses, wise and round,
While gossiping with trees unbound.
They tell of squirrels stealing nuts,
And dance as branches twist their guts.

The pine needles whisper soft and sly,
As rabbits pause and ask them why.
What's so funny in this shade?
"Just pine antics," the trees said.

In this theater of leaf and bark,
Every laugh ignites a spark.
Where all the creatures play and jest,
In woodland life, we find the best.

The Green Heartbeat of the Forest

With every heartbeat, life takes form,
In the foliage, a playful storm.
Mossy carpets tickle the toes,
While branches wave in comical bows.

Fungi giggle, sprouting wide,
As muted whispers play and glide.
The brook hums tunes, a bubbly course,
Inviting all to join the force.

Petals flutter, teasing bees,
While birds chirp jokes on gentle breeze.
Every leaf a chuckle brings,
As unity in laughter sings.

Amidst the green, it's quite the show,
With nature's rhythm and playful flow.
So let us dance in leafy glee,
And share in joy, both wild and free.

Harvesting Melodies from the Boughs

In orchards where the branches sway,
Fruits gather round for a jolly play.
Each apple grins, a cheeky smile,
As friends join in, if just a while.

Harvest moons get on their toes,
While pumpkins wear their best of clothes.
The berries boast of dreams so sweet,
As perfect pairs, they can't be beat.

The wind sings tunes to every bud,
While peas do cartwheels, full of mud.
They laugh at crows who steal and peck,
In this garden, joy's the check.

So grab a basket, join the fun,
The melodies of bounty run.
In every bough, a laugh in store,
Harvest cheer, and let it soar!

Whispers of the Evergreen

In the forest where trees giggle,
Squirrels dance and bugs wiggle.
Branches gossip of silly things,
As the pine cone choir merrily sings.

The owls pretend to be wise sages,
While the raccoons turn all their pages.
Lost in tales of acorns and bark,
Their laughter echoes through the dark.

The Song of the Wind-Bent Trees

The trees twist and twirl in the breeze,
Telling secrets with the greatest of ease.
One tree huffs, another tree puffs,
Chasing shadows, having some laughs.

With branches flailing and leaves aflutter,
They giggle and argue, oh what a clutter!
Mocking the clouds that drift on by,
Making shapes of pumpernickel pies.

Beneath the Canopy's Embrace

Underneath the leafy chatter,
A chipmunk scams for crumbs that scatter.
With tiny paws, he's quite the thief,
Stealing snacks and causing grief.

The ferns sway like they're in a dance,
While beetles try to steal a chance.
To boogie and wiggle their tiny feet,
The forest floor, such a rhythmic treat!

Harmony in the Pine Needles

Pine needles form a ticklish choir,
While spiders weave the dreams they desire.
The trees hum tunes of wild delight,
As rabbits hop and take their flight.

In this festival of laughs galore,
Breezes tickle like never before.
Nature's tricksters in playful spins,
Where the fun never ends, and laughter begins!

The Lure of the Wooded Whispers

In the woods where squirrels dance,
They think they're kings with a nutty chance.
Trees wear gowns of green and brown,
While raccoons steal the show, not a frown.

Branches creak with gossip near,
A woodpecker's peck brings hearty cheer.
Mice munch crumbs that picnic folk drop,
While owls wonder if they should hop.

Toadstools giggle under moon's light,
As fireflies blink in a playful flight.
Nature holds a quirky play,
Where every creature joins the fray.

So if you wander, take a look,
These leafy jesters by the brook.
In the charm of woods, humor weaves,
The laughter in leaves, oh how it leaves!

Chronicles of the Verdant Vale

In a vale where the clovers grow wide,
A snail in a race, oh what a ride!
Frogs croak jokes in a bubbly tone,
While a hedgehog checks his phone.

Bees debate who buzzed last night,
As butterflies flirt in dizzy flight.
In this realm where laughter reigns,
Nature's humor flows like rains.

Rabbits hop in a wobbly way,
Claiming they've got a new dance play.
Each leaf a witness to the fun,
As the sun sets, the giggles run.

Watch the badger carry a hat,
Complaining about the size of that.
In the vale, such tales unfold,
A whimsical world, gleefully bold!

Sylvan Verses at Twilight

By twilight's glow, the trees start to yawn,
As crickets sing a tuneful dawn.
A fox tells tales of old and new,
While the raccoons plot their evening stew.

Mushrooms wear hats that make them proud,
The owls hoot jokes to a gathering crowd.
Twilight breezes whispering laughs,
Nature plays in its quirky halves.

With every glance, a wonder sprouts,
A squirrel dropping acorns, oh the clouts.
The rustling leaves join in the fun,
As stars peek out, the night's begun.

Gather 'round the firefly show,
Where laughter twinkles in a gentle flow.
In sylvan realms, the whimsy grows,
Where every second, a new joke flows!

Nature's Glistening Hymn

In the garden where the daisies wink,
Nature sings, and butterflies think.
A turtle slips, chasing a dream,
While peonies giggle in a gentle stream.

The sun tickles petals, a golden tease,
As locusts hum, aiming to please.
Chickadees chirp with a comedic flair,
Telling tales of great woodland care.

As the breeze carries a playful sound,
Every leaf flutters, joy abound.
Nature's show, a whimsical time,
With laughter echoing in every rhyme.

So amongst the blooms and giant pine,
We find the fun in every line.
In the rhythm of the wild's bright hymn,
Our spirits soar, on a joyful whim!

An Ode to the Ancient Canopy

Up high the branches sway with glee,
A squirrel's dance, a sight to see.
With acorn hats and tiny shoes,
They twirl around as if to cruise.

The leaves whisper secrets, oh so sly,
As chirps and chortles fill the sky.
A bird's quirk, a cat's silly leap,
Nature's mischief, alive and deep.

The shadows play hide and seek with joy,
Tickling toes of every girl and boy.
With laughter ringing, loud and clear,
The ancient woodlands draw us near.

So here's to trees with humor vast,
Their towering tales will always last.
In this great grove where giggles meet,
Nature's jesters cannot be beat.

Voices of the Verdant Woodlands

In leafy whispers, jokes are spun,
The forest's comedians, having fun.
With rustling leaves and bouncing boughs,
They crack up critters, take a bow.

The rabbits chuckle, the deer dance,
Each gust of wind gives life a chance.
A turtle's grin, the fox's sass,
In this green realm, we all amass.

Tree trunks grunt with jovial cheer,
While owls hoot, "Come join us here!"
A picnic planned by ants so small,
A feast for all in the woodland hall.

So roam beneath the boughs so bright,
With every leap, take flight, take flight!
For in this land of green delight,
The woodlands sing with pure delight.

The Spirit of the Pine

Oh Pine, you stand so straight and tall,
Your needles prick, but that's not all.
You tickle noses with your scent,
A playful tease, a nature's jest bent.

The squirrels bounce like they've lost their way,
A acrobatic show just for today!
With nutty giggles, they zoom past,
In the spirit of fun, they'll forever last.

Beneath your branches, shadows play,
Where creatures gather, night or day.
A party forms, with friends so dear,
An arboreal laugh, loud and clear.

So here's to you, oh spunky tree,
With a heart so light, you set us free.
In laughter's embrace, we intertwine,
All thanks to you, great spirit of pine.

Harmonies Beneath the Leafy Dome

Under the canopy, voices blend,
A symphony that will never end.
With rustling hymns and chirping beats,
The forest's song is filled with treats.

A rabbit croons, the fox joins in,
With melodies that surely win.
The owls conduct with a wise old hoot,
While roots tap dance, around the shoot.

Snakes slide smoothly, adding flair,
To the woodland rhymes floating in air.
The dancing leaves join in the fun,
Their twirls and swirls have just begun.

So let us gather as nature thrives,
In a concert where humor survives.
For each note struck beneath the dome,
In harmony, we feel at home.

Nestled Secrets of the Forest Groves

In the woods where whispers dance,
Squirrels wear their pants askew.
A rabbit's got a secret glance,
Hiding snacks, who knew?

The owls declare a mid-night feast,
With bears that waltz in pajamas.
In this furry, leafy beast,
They play Bingo with pyjamas!

Raccoons sing a silly tune,
By moonlight and by firefly.
The forest groove is quite the boon,
As trees twist and sway oh my!

So gather 'round, let's join the cheer,
In nature's laughter, we belong.
With every rustle, every cheer,
In the forest, we sing along.

Rooted in Harmony

The pine trees share a ticklish tale,
Of sap that dripped like candy syrup.
With branches swaying, never frail,
They dance in winds, like happy hiccup!

The acorns chuckle on the ground,
Creating laughter from the floor.
A nutty rhythm all around,
The forest's beat, we all adore!

A family of frogs starts to croak,
In perfect time, a crazy jam.
'Tis nature's joke, a funny poke,
Here in this woodland, we all scram.

So if you stroll through leafy lanes,
Join in the fun, don't be shy!
For in these woods, where joy reigns,
A giggle's gold, and oh so spry!

The Melancholy of Fallen Leaves

Oh, how the leaves complain and sigh,
As they tumble down from the tree.
"Why must we leave?" they often cry,
"The ground is no place to be free!"

They gossip as they twist mid-air,
Debating if they'd rather float.
Some dream of breezes and fresh air,
While others just want to stay and gloat.

A squirrel nearby rolls in their pile,
Flipping and flopping in delight.
Wishing to join in their style,
The leaves grumble, "What a sight!"

But soon laughs fill the autumn day,
As friends they find beneath the boughs.
In every drift and every sway,
They learn to smile, forget their woes.

From Foliage to Forest Floor

From the tallest bough to the ground below,
Laughter echoes, twirls, and sways.
A swinging vine puts on a show,
As monkeys join in, they play!

Down through the leaves, a tickle-treat,
A hedgehog rolls with fussy glee.
With prickles out, it's quite the feat,
He rolls around, "Look at me!"

A raccoon with a mask so sly,
Finding treasures, oh so bold.
Making mischief, oh my, oh my!
Nature's drama, simply gold!

So frolic, dance, enjoy the jest,
In woods where giggles bloom and beam.
For in this forest, at its best,
We ride the wave of a happy dream!

Enveloping Shadows of the Evergreens

In the shade of a tall green friend,
Squirrels plot and pretzel bend.
A raccoon steals a sandwich quick,
While a mockingbird sings a silly trick.

The branches sway, they dance and creak,
The mischief here is quite unique.
A laughing log rolls down the hill,
As whispers float with comedic thrill.

A deer wears sunglasses, posing proud,
As if to say, "Look at me, I'm loud!"
With every rustle, a giggle grows,
In the forest's heart, where humor flows.

So come and join this wooded crew,
For laughter blooms where the tall trees grew.
The giants watch with knowing grins,
As the fun in the mossy ground begins.

The Poetry of Pine and Spirit

In the realm where tall pines sway,
A chipmunk jives, hip-hop all day.
The owls hoot out their best beats,
While rabbits tap dance on their feets.

Beneath the branches, shadows play,
A wise old tree starts to ballet.
It twirls around with roots so grand,
That even the fungi give a hand.

The pinecones chuckle as they drop,
Creating melodies that never stop.
With pine-scented giggles in the air,
The forest fills with joy to share.

So gather 'round for a hoedown spree,
Among the trees where spirits are free.
Each tree tells tales of whimsical worth,
In a poetry dance beneath the earth.

Whispers of the Evergreen

In a whispering grove so green,
Trees gossip about the unseen.
"Did you hear what the brook just said?"
A pine smirks, "Sounds like gossip spread!"

The squirrels share snacks of acorn pie,
While the woodpeckers join in the high fly.
"Your branch is looking quite bough-tiful,"
One tree winks, feeling quite youthful.

A bush bursts out in flowing laughter,
As the winds howl, chasing after.
The forest floor hums a merry tune,
Under the watch of a giggling moon.

So let's take time to laugh and breathe,
In this sanctuary where tales weave.
With every rustle and every cheer,
These whispers craft a joy sincere.

Songs from the Ancient Grove

From the depths of the ancient wood,
Elders sing in a rhythm understood.
With barky voices, they croon and prance,
Inviting all to join in the dance.

A tap-dancing beetle leads the way,
With a shimmy that brightens the gray.
As sunbeams twinkle through leafy folds,
The hilarity of nature boldly unfolds.

"Do you have any pine-flavored jokes?"
Chortles the tree, "Let's share some pokes!"
With a riddle here and a pun over there,
The ancient grove fills with tender care.

So marvel at these tall storytellers,
Their quirky tales and delightful hellers.
In their laughter and music, find your bliss,
For in this grove, no humor's amiss.

Twilight's Embrace in the Glade

In the glade, where shadows play,
A squirrel juggles nuts all day.
He drops one and gives a shout,
"Guess that nut was full of clout!"

Fireflies dance with twinkling lights,
Chasing each other, what a sight!
A rabbit joins, with hops so spry,
"Catch me if you can!" he'll cry.

The owls hoot with a sage-like tone,
While crickets laugh at being alone.
A bear arrives, with a goofy grin,
"Who knew night could be so much fun?"

The moon above, a big round pie,
Glistens down with a gleeful eye.
Laughter echoes through the trees,
Nature sings, as we join in glee.

The Nature Walk's Gentle Rhythm

On a path, where leaves do rustle,
A hedgehog plays, oh what a hustle!
He rolls into a bush so wide,
"Guess I'll take a leafy slide!"

Birds chirp, making quite a fuss,
While weaving tales without a bus.
A turtle strolls, slow as can be,
"Hurry up, or you'll miss the tea!"

A deer leaps in, with grace and style,
"I'll show you all how to run a mile!"
But trips on roots, and takes a fall,
Laughter rings through nature's hall.

The sun dips low, painting the sky,
As frogs start singing, oh my, oh my!
With giggles from critters, a wacky show,
Nature's humor steals the glow.

The Green Symphony at Dusk

As dusk descends, the frogs commence,
A concert loud, with little sense.
"Ribbit, ribbit, join my crew!"
Their band of joy is quite the view.

Trees sway gently in the breeze,
As squirrels practice their stand-up tease.
One drops a nut, the crowd erupts,
Even the owl can't hold his chucks!

A raccoon struts, his mask on tight,
"I'm the star of the night's delight!"
With a twist and turn, he steals the scene,
Twirling wildly, oh look at him preen!

As stars twinkle in the night's great book,
Nature laughs with every nook.
In this symphony, so rich and grand,
The woods unite, a silly band.

Ephemeral Echoes of the Vale

In the vale, where whispers dwell,
A goat starts singing, oh so well!
"Baah-rilliant talent!" says a sheep,
As everyone giggles, in a heap.

The fog rolls in, a cloak of fun,
A crafty fox shouts, "Let's all run!"
But trips and tumbles right away,
"Looks like I need a dance class today!"

A parrot mimics all the ruckus,
"Sounds so silly, can't you focus?"
With antics shared, the laughter swells,
Echoing through the trees and knells.

Stars blink down, with a cheeky grin,
As creatures toast to another win.
In this vale of giggles and cheer,
Nature delights, year after year.

Notes of the High Canopy

In the branches, squirrels dance,
They wear tiny boots, take a chance.
Chasing each other, up and down,
Who knew trees would host a clown?

Birds chirp jokes, like stand-up pros,
Cracking puns with every dose.
A raccoon laughs, holding his gut,
"Why do branches always strut?"

In leafy gossip, the leaves unite,
Sharing tales from morning to night.
A woodpecker taps a rhythm so sweet,
While ants in formation dance to the beat.

With each wind's gust, the humor flies,
Nature's laughter, what a surprise!
So if you listen, lean in and see,
Joy lives high up in the green jubilee.

Fables of the Evergreens

Tall tales weave through emerald halls,
Where pinecone princes throw grand balls.
The owl's a joker, wise and sly,
With punchlines that make the branches sigh.

A fox in a hat struts with great flair,
Swapping stories without a care.
"Have you heard the one 'bout the sap?"
"It's sticky, my friend, just take a nap!"

The shadows giggle, playing their game,
Underneath those evergreen frames.
"Why don't trees compete in the race?"
"We'd leaf 'em behind, it's not our place!"

As the moonlight spills over the lane,
The forest chuckles, life's simple gain.
In these fables, fun takes flight,
Evergreens know how to hold the night.

A Chorus Among the Pines

Pines sway with rhythm, a tuneful scene,
Branches clapping, evergreen keen.
"Why did the twig refuse to bend?"
"Too many branches end up as trends!"

The wind joins in, with a whistling call,
As pine needles drop, they dance down the hall.
"Leaf me alone!" shouts a weary branch,
But the others just laugh, not a chance!

A chipmunk sings about forgotten nuts,
While beetles tap dance in tiny ruts.
"Hey, nature! Do you know the score?"
"Just branch out, there's always more!"

In this leafy choir, all find their tune,
Jokes float like pollen, beneath the moon.
So when you wander through these greens,
Remember the laughter, the joyous scenes.

The Reminiscence of Old Growth

An ancient oak chuckles with pride,
Telling stories of the paths he's tried.
"Back in my day, we grew so tall,
We'd shade a whole village, I recall!"

"Remember the squirrel who stole my hat?
Gave him a wedgie, what of that?"
Fungi giggle, joining the verse,
"Old growth's wisdom isn't a curse!"

A bear walks by, snorting with glee,
"Got lost, but the trees guided me."
He shares his tales of yesterday's fun,
While mossy carpets soak up the sun.

With laughter blending through the leaves,
Old stories dance in the gentle breeze.
So listen closely, if you dare,
To the wisdom hidden in the air.

Odes to the Stalwart Spruce

In the forest where the fun starts,
Stalwart spruce plays many parts.
Dancing squirrels swing by the leaves,
Tickled branches, laughter weaves.

Birds think they're great stand-up acts,
With silly jokes and funny facts.
The bark listens, no need for applause,
Rooted deep, it laughs without cause.

Sunshine glints upon their bristles,
While pine cones fall, oh what a missle!
A chipmunk slips on dew-kissed ground,
Impromptu flips, a show profound!

Oh stalwart spruce, you make us grin,
With every breeze, the joy within.
In your shade, we chuckle and share,
Life's silly moments, floating in air.

Serenades in the Silent Knoll

In the knoll where whispers play,
Trees join in a funny ballet.
A gopher dons a tiny hat,
While dancing mice go tit for tat.

The shade, a stage for creatures small,
A concert where the shadows sprawl.
An owl hoots an awkward tune,
As crickets join beneath the moon.

Frogs croak out their grand debut,
With harmonies, they sing anew.
The wind chuckles, sways along,
Joining in their playful song.

Oh Silent Knoll, your antics bright,
With every giggle, pure delight.
Nature's jesters in the green,
In this place, we sow the scene.

Twilight Interlude Among the Needles

At twilight's edge, the needled friends,
Greet the night that never ends.
Whispers of mischief fill the air,
As shadows stretch from here to there.

A raccoon juggles acorns gay,
While owls snicker in their way.
The moon chuckles at the sight,
Of furry chums in fading light.

Needles sway as the giggles rise,
In moonlit skits beneath the skies.
With every rustle, a clever jest,
The forest's laughter, oh how blessed!

In twilight's hold, the moments gleam,
Nature's laughter, a joyful dream.
Among the needles, pure delight,
A symphony of silly sight.

Reverberations of the Wooded Realm

In the realm where the trees engage,
A leafy stage, each turn a page.
The boughs shake with a chuckle free,
Singing songs from tree to tree.

Squirrels scamper with a flair,
Sprouting jokes upon the air.
The brook joins in with giggling tones,
While frogs croak out their puns in drones.

Each breeze whispers a playful tease,
Rolling laughter through the leaves.
The trunk knocks back with gentle thuds,
A symphony of wood and buds.

Reverberate, oh merry grove,
In rib-tickling stories, we will rove.
Life's a riot when trees can play,
In this realm of fun, we'll stay.

Roots of Resonance

In the forest, trees do sway,
Roots are dancing, come what may.
Squirrels giggle, jump so high,
While wise owls watch and sigh.

Rabbits hop in silly pairs,
Twisting branches, joyful flares.
With every rustle, laughter's near,
A symphony we love to hear.

The log's a stage for frogs to croak,
With punchlines that make the pines choke.
As the breeze tunes up the show,
Nature's funny, don't you know?

Roots embrace a soft, wild jest,
Nature's laughter, truly blessed.
Every moment, pure delight,
In the forest, all feels right.

The Forest's Soft Refrain

Beneath the boughs, the whispers flow,
As chipmunks chuckle, stealing the show.
A breeze will tickle, leaves will dance,
In this trio, all take a chance.

A deer prances, wearing a crown,
While others giggle, spreading around.
With sunlit beams, they'll lose all care,
Forest tunes in the crisp night air.

Snakes with swagger slide on by,
Witty jokes, oh my, oh my!
Counting echoes, one, two, three,
Nature's joke, come join the spree.

From the tallest pine, a laugh so sweet,
In unity, all creatures meet.
Singing melodies, spirits fly,
Life is fun as time slips by.

Songs of the Canopy Creatures

Up in branches, where critters play,
Squirrels sing, they twist and sway.
Bees buzz tunes, oh what a scene,
While raccoons snicker, oh so mean!

High above, the branches sway,
A comedy show in sunlight's ray.
Cardinals chirp a silly song,
Even the insects hum along.

Parrots boast with a vibrant flair,
Jokes exchanged in twirling air.
Chasing shadows, smart and spry,
In this realm, laughter flies high.

Canopies hosting wondrous glee,
Nature's charm, wild and free.
Each song an echo, each laugh a cheer,
Together we sing, year after year.

Under the Watchful Green

Beneath the leaves, secrets we keep,
Laughter bubbles, never too steep.
With every rustle, joy we find,
Under the watchful, playful kind.

A hedgehog rolls, a moment's bliss,
While wise old trees watch with a hiss.
Pigeons cooing, join the fun,
As shadows dance in the setting sun.

Frogs croak echoes, jokes in sync,
Mice debate on how to wink.
The forest hums a hearty tune,
As daylight fades, we laugh 'til noon.

Under the green, a merry throng,
Where nature sings a wild, sweet song.
In every breeze, a giggle stirs,
In leafy halls, joy reoccur.

Nature's Chorus of Solitude

In the trees, the squirrels chatter,
About the latest rumors, what's the matter.
The raccoons in tuxedos dance with glee,
While the owls roll their eyes, sipping herbal tea.

Frogs play jazz on lily pads so bright,
While crickets keep time in the fading light.
A rabbit juggles carrots, with a grin,
As the moon leans down, inviting them in.

Echoing Through the Hollowed Pines

The pines whisper jokes from tree to tree,
Even the wind can't help but agree.
A deer tells a tale, its laughter loud,
While a snail slides by, far too proud.

Bats swoop low, joining the fun,
Creating a ruckus, 'til the day is done.
The owls chuckle, in their evening dress,
As the stars twinkle back, saying, 'You're just a mess!'

Silhouettes Against the Eastern Glow

The sun peeks up, it's a rude affair,
The critters groan, 'Do we have to care?'
A fox yawns wide, stretching out its paws,
While a lark prepares, with endless applause.

Squirrels debate, who has the best stash,
While chipmunks join in, all ready to clash.
They tumble and tumble, in this morning's thrill,
While the spiders watch, plotting their next drill.

Timbered Melodies of Dusk

As twilight falls, the trees start to sway,
With catchy tunes that lead them astray.
A family of foxes puts on a show,
With twirls and leaps, they're stealing the glow.

Bats hum a tune, oh, what a sight!
Confusing the frogs, who are ready to fight.
And amidst it all, a hedgehog balled tight,
Dreams of the dance that might take flight.

Ballad of the Wandering Roots

In a forest where the branches sway,
Roots decided to dance and play.
They twirled beneath the twilight glow,
But tangled up with weeds, oh no!

A squirrel laughed at their ballet,
He flipped and flopped in merry dismay.
The roots complained of their rough fate,
"Who knew soil could be such a weight?"

They formed a band, a wacky troupe,
Playing music with a silly whoop.
The earthworms joined for a funky beat,
The forest echoed with their funky feat.

So if you hear the earth's merry cheer,
Just know the roots are dancing here.
In laughter, they find their funny groove,
Amidst the trees, they still love to move.

Shadows of the Timeless Grove

Underneath the shady trees,
Lurks a fox who likes to tease.
In shades of green, he makes his play,
Whispering secrets that lead astray.

The owl hoots, with a twinkle bright,
"I'll be the judge; boys, don't you fight!"
While echoing giggles come from below,
As raccoons and rabbits join in the show.

With shadows dancing on the ground,
The mischief spreads, it knows no bounds.
A conga line of critters so spry,
Wobbling round, oh my, oh my!

The grove resounds with joyous cheer,
Every critter sidesteps all fear.
In the timeless shadows, they frolic free,
Creating a ruckus, just wait and see!

Reverie of the Sylvan Sigh

A tree with dreams began to sway,
Wishing on leaves for a funny day.
He chuckled as the wind blew by,
"If trees could laugh, I'd never cry!"

The birds got wind of the grand affair,
And flapped their wings without a care.
They hatched a plan, a wild parade,
With acorns and berries, a sweet charade!

Beneath the branches, the forest's vibe,
Animals danced, oh what a tribe!
With rainbows splashing through every smile,
They skipped and jumped with endless style.

In this reverie, laughter took flight,
As twilight painted the trees in light.
With every giggle, the night grew bright,
A symphony of joy, a starry delight!

Murmurs in the Mountains Green

Whispers float on the mountain breeze,
Of funny antics and clumsy knees.
A goat in shades tried a little stunt,
But rolled down laughing, a comical front.

The squirrels chattered, plotting a game,
Who can climb up and shout their name?
With every tumble and playful slip,
The trees erupted, joy on their lip.

A bear with berries danced in delight,
While the rabbits hopped, a merry sight.
The mountains echoed with wondrous sounds,
As nature's laughter spun round and round.

Murmurs of mirth live on in the glen,
As friends gather in the sun once again.
With trickster tales woven through the leaves,
In this mountain playground, everyone believes!

The Rustic Chorus of Winter

In the forest, a snowman grins,
Whispering secrets of winter wins.
The squirrels debate, who's the best?
As snowflakes fall, they jest and jest.

The owls hoot in their fluffy coats,
While rabbits hop, wearing funny floats.
With each frosty moment, laughter grows,
In this woodland stage, where humor flows.

Icicles dangle like frozen spears,
As trees dance lightly, devoid of fears.
A merry tune, the wind does play,
In this winter realm, we laugh all day.

So raise a branch, give winter a cheer,
Join in the fun, there's nothing to fear.
With giggles echoing, trees sway loud,
In the rustic chorus, we're all so proud.

Battle Hymn of the Bark

In the woods, a fight for air,
Bark beetles march, without a care.
The trees proclaim, "Protect your skin!"
As tiny soldiers prepare to win.

The fungi chuckle, they're in the mix,
Cheering for both with their cunning tricks.
"Who knew a bug could bring such flair?"
In this bark battle, it's perfect wear!

Amidst the tussles, the birds all cheer,
Singing of triumphs, lending an ear.
With branches clapping in rhythm, it seems,
Nature's own chorus, fulfilling our dreams.

So gather 'round, all critters unite,
In this barky brawl, we take our flight.
With laughter soaring, the forest alights,
In the battle hymn, joy ignites.

Nomads of the Wooded Realm

What a sight, the squirrels flee,
Hauling acorns, carefree glee!
In this leafy world, they're on the roam,
With funny tails, they build their home.

The raccoons laugh in circus bands,
Juggling nuts with their tiny hands.
"Look at us!" they shout with pride,
In this wooded realm, we take joyride.

The foxes prance in a frolicsome dance,
Chasing shadows, giving chance a chance.
With a grin and a wink, they plot and scheme,
Being nomads here is the ultimate dream.

So come along, join this merry troop,
In the wilderness, we form a loop.
With each step taken, laughter we weave,
In the wooded realm, we forever believe.

A Journey Through Leaves and Light

Through rustling leaves, we take our flight,
In this sun-drenched world, everything's bright.
The butterflies giggle, flapping high,
While bumblebees buzz and ask, "Why?"

Under the trees, a dance starts to spin,
The foliage rustles, come join in!
With each turn and twist, we break into cheer,
In this playful journey, let's draw near.

The sunlight paints patterns on our way,
Creating shadows where we love to play.
"Follow me!" shouts a hedgehog in rhyme,
In this leafy labyrinth, we move in time.

So wander with us, through light and shade,
In this joyous journey, no moment will fade.
With laughter as music, we dance and glide,
In this whimsical world, let fun be our guide.

Resounding Silence of the Pines

In the deep woods, whispers reign,
Tall trees start to complain.
Squirrels laugh as they conspire,
Plotting how to steal a tire.

Mice with hats and sneaky feet,
Conceive a plan quite neat.
They nod and cheer, their voices soar,
While owls shake their heads in lore.

Creaking branches join the fun,
Nature's joke has just begun.
But here's the truth, I must confess,
It's the trees who wear the stress!

Beneath the moon, shadows prance,
Frisky critters join the dance.
With twinkling stars, a comical sight,
Pines chuckle softly through the night.

Serenades of the Fabled Forest

In a forest, odd and bold,
Trees gossip secrets untold.
With giggles that echo through the glade,
They share the tales of the decisions made.

Fairies flutter, ticker-tape run,
Sprinkling sparkles, having fun.
With ants in top hats, elegant line,
They march to a tune, and it's quite divine!

Bears with banjos, squirrels with flutes,
Join the ball in their furry suits.
The mushrooms clap, the owls roll their eyes,
As nature bursts out in laughter and sighs.

As dawn breaks, the joke floats high,
Grass blades giggle – oh my, oh my!
In the fabled forest, with laughter rife,
Even the logs seem to have a life!

The Dance of the Wood Spirits

In midnight woods where shadows play,
Wood spirits frolic, come what may.
They trip and stumble, find their feet,
With vines for ties, it's quite the feat!

A log rolls by with a wink and nod,
While crickets chirp – it's not so odd.
With twirling leaves, they spin and slide,
Grab your partner, it's time to glide!

Raccoons juggle berries in a line,
While trees shake limbs, how simply divine!
The party writes its own decree,
Who knew wood spirits had such glee?

As dawn approaches, the laughter fades,
Silent pines stand like serenades.
But next moonrise, you can bet your shoes,
The woods will dance – they refuse to snooze!

Twilight's Embrace Among the Trees

When twilight falls and shadows bloom,
The trees throw parties, fill the room.
A moose in shades, a fox in style,
Say, 'Stay a while, give us a smile!'

The wind sings tunes of ancient bazaars,
While raccoons plan for moonlit bars.
Bottles of dew, and nut-filled plates,
An invitation that celebrates fates!

Owls with monocles offer views,
While squirrels shake a little snooze.
Underneath stars that twinkle and wink,
Everyone sighs, "Let's have a drink!"

But as they toast with acorn cups,
The trees chuckle; they've seen it all up.
With whispers of breeze, they sway and tease,
'Let's dance away on this playful breeze!'

Chants of the Timberland

In the woods where squirrels leap,
They plan their mischief, not to sleep.
With acorns flying, a game of tag,
Who knew that trees could start to brag?

The raccoons dance with flair and style,
While owls hoot and wear a smile.
A twig's a mic, the bark's a stage,
Woodland antics, all the rage!

Frogs croak loud, they sing off-key,
As crickets join in harmony.
In this forest, laughter flows,
Nature's jesters, as everyone knows.

So raise a toast to this mad spree,
Where every tree holds a memory.
Laughter echoes, the night is bright,
In timberland, every day's a delight!

The Swaying Soliloquy

In the breeze, the branches jig,
A wobbly dance, oh so big!
Leaves are tickled by a prankster air,
Giggling trees, everywhere!

The roots complain, they're stuck in place,
While trunks wiggle at a silly pace.
Buds blossom with a cheeky grin,
Nature's laughter, let's join in!

A pigeon struts, thinking it's grand,
He trips on twigs, slips in the sand.
With every flap, he shakes the ground,
And chuckles follow his flight around.

So sway along with nature's cheer,
Feel the joy that we hold dear.
One-two-step with every branch,
In this dance, let's take a chance!

Voices of the Aromatic Bastion

In a forest rich with scent and sound,
The trees converse, their roots unbound.
Whispers of pine and cedar bold,
In this realm, secrets unfold.

A skunk recounts tales of the night,
While fireflies blink with delight.
Maples giggle, like caffeinated fools,
Sharing stories of woodland schools.

"Hey there, buddy!" a beech tree shouts,
As a deer prances and loudly doubts.
With every tickle of the grassy floor,
They joke about the sun's daily chore.

So gather 'round, let laughter bloom,
In this fragrant, leafy room.
Nature's chatter brightens the day,
Where every creature finds their play.

Nature's Rustic Requiem

The winds whirl soft with playful glee,
As branches sway, oh so carefree.
A woodpecker taps a snappy beat,
While vines twirl like they're on repeat.

With frogs composing a raucous tune,
Under the light of a silvery moon.
Mushrooms laugh, they've raised a toast,
To every critter, they love the most.

The nightingale croons an off-pitch song,
As bees buzz in, where they belong.
Drunk on nectar, flowers sway,
They dance around in a bright bouquet.

So come and join, don't miss the fun,
In nature's antics, we've all won.
With laughter echoing through the trees,
Let's celebrate with the wildest ease!

www.ingramcontent.com/pod-product-compliance
Lightning Source LLC
Chambersburg PA
CBHW071840160426
43209CB00003B/361